Artful
Mini Cards™

By Janice E. McKee

Contents

Artful Mini Cards

EDITOR Tanya Fox

CREATIVE DIRECTOR Brad Snow

PUBLISHING SERVICES DIRECTOR Brenda Gallmeyer

MANAGING EDITOR Brooke Smith

COPY SUPERVISOR Deborah Morgan

COPY EDITORS Emily Carter, Rebecca Detwiler

TECHNICAL EDITOR Corene Painter

PHOTOGRAPHY SUPERVISOR Tammy Christian

PHOTO STYLISTS Tammy Liechty, Tammy Steiner

PHOTOGRAPHY Matthew Owen

PRODUCTION ARTIST SUPERVISOR Erin Brandt

PRODUCTION ARTIST Nicole Gage

PRODUCTION ASSISTANTS Marj Morgan, Judy Neuenschwander

ISBN: 978-1-59635-377-0
Printed in USA
1 2 3 4 5 6 7 8 9

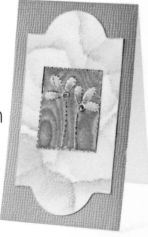

blossom

4

Foreword

Sometimes my husband, David, takes his lunch to work. In the past ten years or so, he has found little love notes from me in the form of miniature cards when he opens his brown paper sack. Reluctant to throw them out, he started collecting them in a drawer in his desk. Soon the cards were taking up too much space. David then bought a bulletin board to put up on one of his office walls so he could hang the ever-growing stack of cards there. It became a conversation piece and the inspiration for this book.

At first, I made miniature cards in order to use up my leftovers from other card-making projects. Much thought and care was taken to create a small art piece to act as the perfect gift card for a package. Now, I find them to be just as intriguing and entertaining to make as larger cards. With the 12 different tutorials found in this book, as well as the numerous samples shown, I hope you will be inspired to fashion your own little works of art for any number of occasions.

The techniques discussed here range from monoprinting and working with rice paper to incorporating fabric and hand-stitching onto mini cards. In addition to tried-and-true methods such as rubber stamping, newer ideas, such as working with artfully printed paper napkins, are shown. This book will send you to the garden to collect botanical specimens for pressed-flower cards as well as remind you to check out the past for vintage images that work well in card making. It's fun and worth exploring.

About the Author

I was born in Louisiana and have been a resident of Texas much of my adult life. I've been married to my wonderful husband, David, for over 35 years. We are the parents of four dear children: Marc, Meaghan, Roane and Donald (and love our daughter-in-law, Camellia).

I've been interested in paper since the age of 5 or 6—whenever a relative would give me a quarter, I'd head to the dime store to buy a little writing tablet or pack of paper. A few years later, fabric came into my line of sight in learning to make doll clothes. Of course, I'd always enjoyed paper dolls too.

After learning to make garments in high school home ec, I majored in Home Economics in college. Sewing clothes for the family, making quilts and experimenting with embroidery were all a creative joy for me. In the 1990s, I became interested in nature crafts and papermaking, which led to card making. It's been exciting and fun all along the way.

Coloring Rice Paper

"Imagination is the beginning of creation. You imagine what you desire, you will what you imagine and at last you create what you will."

—George Bernard Shaw

When I was experimenting with creating handmade paper back in the '90s—the kind that's made from recycled gift wrap, unused fast food napkins, credit card offers, etc. (torn and turned into pulp in a household blender)—nearly every type of plant matter was fair game. In addition to the usual flower petals and grasses, I tried overripe strawberries, pine needles, cantaloupe rinds and the tough ends of asparagus stalks. While not everything produced great-looking paper, there were enough successes (loved the blueberry paper!) to inspire further experimentation.

At one point, while looking in the refrigerator for possibilities, I spied some leftover rice. I'd heard of rice paper but had never actually seen or used it. "Why not?" I thought to myself.

Let me just say: Do not try this at home! It was a disaster. The goopy mess adhered to my screen and couching sheets like glue and absolutely would not form itself into a sheet of paper. Months later I read somewhere that "rice" paper was actually a misnomer as the paper had nothing to do with rice.

Well, that is not exactly true. According to www.rice-paper.com, original rice paper had its beginnings in the Tang Dynasty (A.D. 618–907) and was made from rice straw and wingceltis bark in the Xuancheng area of China. It was known as Xuancheng paper and was valued by calligraphers and sumi-e artists for its strength and durability.

"One of the special characters of the paper is that it is rotproof and mothproof. This is the reason why an artwork from 100 years ago can still have its original freshness," so declares the website.

I've only worked with rice paper for a couple of years, but it is indeed a wonderful paper. It has qualities that remind me of cloth. For one, it is easily torn and yet its strength allows for quite a bit of manipulation. Another benefit is that once the decorated paper is dry it will usually lie flat, instead of curling up as other papers do.

Here are a few ideas to try, including a materials list.

Materials

Rice paper	Spray sizing (optional)
Acrylic paint	Freezer paper
Inks	Paintbrushes
Spray paint	Sea sponges
Spray bottle filled with water	Bamboo skewer (optional)
Various objects such as ferns, floral petals, cut-out paper shapes and stencils	Aluminum foil
	Iron
	Oven
	Temporary adhesive

Note: *Cover work surface with freezer paper. When thinning acrylic paint with water, the paint should have the consistency of whole milk.*

Sponging

Spritz a sheet of rice paper with water. Using a natural sea sponge moistened with water, dip sponge into three coordinated colors of watered-down acrylic paint. Press sponge onto rice paper, pressing down and allowing the colors to spread out. Spritz with more water to make the colors mix as desired.

Modified Marbling

Use water to dilute three or four coordinated colors of acrylic paint.

Make a puddle with one color in the center of work space. Add other colors in the puddle as desired. Use the end of a paintbrush or a bamboo skewer to swirl paint colors. Do not overmix.

Carefully lay the rice paper on top of the puddle and watch the colors spread.

This method begs for experimentation. Allow the rice paper to dry partially before lifting it away. If you move the paper too soon the colors may run in streaks, but perhaps that look will be just what you desire.

Creasing

Crease the rice paper as if making a paper fan. Apply thinned acrylic paints or inks to the creases. Spritz the creases with water as needed to make the paint move. Once dry, unfold and iron flat. If the result is boring, try creasing the paper again, either offsetting the creases or creasing in the other direction.

Using Aluminum Foil

Slightly crumple a piece of aluminum foil that is a little larger than the rice paper you are painting. Smooth the foil out and lay the rice paper on top. Spritz with water, and then paint the paper using a brush or sponge with as many colors of thinned acrylic paint as desired. To speed the drying process, place foil with the paper in an oven set at about 250 degrees for 5–10 minutes. The colors will migrate to the creases in the foil and the results are amazing.

A similar look can be achieved by spritzing the rice paper with water until quite damp and then crumpling it up into a ball.

Slightly uncrumple it and paint as desired.

Again, the paint will seep to the creases and surprise you when it is dry.

Spray Paint

Paint a sheet of rice paper with one or more light colors of thinned acrylic paint; let dry. Next, using a temporary adhesive, adhere objects such as ferns, flower petals, stencils or cut-out paper shapes to the painted sheet. In a well-ventilated area, or outside, using a protected surface and surroundings, lightly spray the paper with spray paint in another color. When dry, remove adhered objects.

These ideas just scratch the surface of what can be achieved when coloring or decorating rice paper. I always prefer to iron my decorated papers once they are dry, applying spray sizing (the same that is used for clothing) as I iron—it gives a nice finish.

Tips

Try using a heat tool to speed up drying time.

Iron dry paper to give it a smooth finished look.

Paper Napkin Images

> *"Plan out your life on paper but live by your heart."*
>
> —Warren DeMike

What comes to mind when you think of paper napkins? Potlucks and picnics? Everyday meals at home? Grabbing fast food on the run in your car? Jotting down an address, song idea or poem on the spur of the moment? How about paper arts and card making? If the last question has never occurred to you, it should! Decorative paper napkins are a great source of artistry and inspiration for making your own paper-art creations.

Crafting with paper napkins has several advantages. They are inexpensive and often showcase beautiful artwork ranging from classic designs to fun party motifs. They are very thin and easily incorporated into backgrounds for cards. Their decorative elements work well in collages or, when supported, can become a focal point. In fact, paper napkins can be utilized in almost any way that other decorative papers are used.

Decorative paper napkins usually come in two- or three-ply form. First, iron the napkin carefully on a low setting to get rid of any creases, and then separate the layers.

While the top, printed layer is what you are most interested in using, do not discard the other layers. The sheet right under the inked top sheet often has a subtle coloring that can be used whole or in part for backgrounds. Any subsequent white layers could make a contribution as pulp for handmade paper. Or, because the layers are extremely thin and therefore somewhat translucent, a white layer can be adhered on top of other gaudy or too dark decorative or scrapbooking papers to either tone them down or lighten them up.

The napkin layers are extremely delicate. The easiest way to add strength and support is to iron them to the shiny side of freezer paper. The resulting piece of paper can now be used as any other textweight paper: as a background sheet or cut up for collage elements.

Designs from paper napkins can be carefully cut out or torn to use as paper appliqués.

Another way to strengthen the decorated layer is to brayer it onto a piece of paper or cardstock that has been run through a Xyron adhesive machine.

The printed napkin layer can be torn and decoupaged using matte medium.

Carefully adhere torn piece of napkin to card front.

Decide on the placement of the torn piece and apply the medium to the foundation of paper, cardstock or cloth.

Alternatively, the torn part can be carefully coated on the backside with a glue stick and adhered to other handmade background papers such as crinkled, watercolored waxed paper.

Carefully lay the napkin piece on top. Taking great care to not tear this delicate piece, gently apply the matte medium on top with a soft paintbrush.

The reverse side of the printed layer will be much more subtle and might provide an interesting coloration upon which to rubber stamp an image such as a face. Different design portions from several napkins can be combined to create a scene. Specific motifs might be applied using adhesive foam dots to give a slightly 3-D effect. Needle-nose tweezers are a great tool to use for handling delicate, small elements.

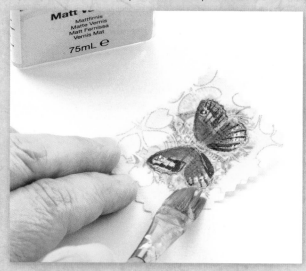

A strengthened napkin layer can take additional color and shading from colored pencils or pastels. After trying a few of these techniques, you might find yourself in party shops, gift shops, drug stores and online stores searching out decorative paper napkins. There is a lot of great art out there just waiting for you.

Once everything has dried, the napkin will be stronger and other ephemera can be added as desired.

Embellished Fabric

"We live in a web of ideas, a fabric of our own making."

—Joseph Chilton Pearce

Ahhh, fabric ... one of my first loves in the creative world. When I was about 9 years old, my grandmother bought me my first fashion doll. She also included in her gift a few garments for the doll. My doll, who was quite the fashion maven, soon needed more outfits. My mother kindly pitched in and made some clothes for my doll. Soon, I pestered her for more, and she suggested that I learn to sew. She taught me a few hand stitches, and with her leftover fabric scraps and thread, I was on my way to a love of sewing. Somehow the baby dolls I'd had previously never inspired such endeavors, but this fashion doll certainly did. When I finally was able to take home economics in high school and learned to use a sewing machine, the first pattern I chose was a dress with a collar, patch pockets and set-in sleeves. Sewing garments led to quiltmaking in later years. I've dabbled in fabric painting too. There is a large closet in our basement that contains multiple shelves of fashion fabrics, quilting fabrics, home decor fabrics and all kinds of scraps.

Happily, fabric has worked its way into card making too, which is another favorite pastime. These miniature cards show that even the smallest scrap of fabric can achieve special notice. So don't throw out those bits and pieces leftover from dressmaking, quilting or home decor projects—just put them to good use in cards and paper-arts projects.

If you do not sew at home, thus lacking your own scraps of cloth, try fabric stores or garage sales for remnants. There are also online sources, such as clotilde.com, where bundles of a variety of fabrics cut in small sizes called Charm Packs, Jelly Rolls or Layer Cakes can be purchased. Retaining the "good parts" of clothing ready to be discarded can work too.

One of my favorite ways to use a scrap piece of fabric for a small card is to create fringed edges all around. By pulling a thread on each lengthwise and crosswise side of the fabric, you will start the unraveling process. Keep pulling threads until the depth of fringe desired is achieved.

Try using pinking shears to create a decorative edge that won't fray.

Hemming the edges by hand or machine will create a clean finish for fabric to be used as a background. An alternative method would be to cut a piece of cardstock the desired finished size for your mini card. Cut your fabric scrap about ⅜ inch larger than the cardstock. Center the cardstock on the fabric and glue down with a glue stick. Flip it over and trim the corners of the fabric to within 1/16 inch at the corner of the cardstock.

Finger-press the raw edges of the fabric over the edges of the cardstock to bring them to the back side. Using a glue stick, glue in place permanently.

Pre-cut wooden shapes or chipboard can be used in place of cardstock. The fabric is then glued to the top of the piece with the raw edges brought to the back and glued down in the same manner as the previous example.

Now that fabric foundations have been prepared for the small cards, it is time to add embellishments. Pressed flowers and motifs cut from decorative paper napkins work well. **Note:** *See section on Paper Napkins on pages 10–13.*

Beads, spangles, sequins, jewelry findings and purchased fabric embellishments, such as ribbon roses, can be added to your mini card for a unique touch.

Ribbon scraps count as fabric too. Wide ribbons can be used for backgrounds while narrower pieces act as enhancements. Ribbons or ribbon-type yarns can also be wrapped around chipboard frames.

Small paper images cut from decoupage sheets, decorative cardstock or scrapbooking paper, drawer liner paper or gift wrap work very well. Use your computer to print out a childhood photo onto muslin for a sweet look.

Don't forget about deconstruction. When fraying or fringing the edges of a piece of fabric to be used as a background, save the threads and tie them together to make the perfect matching bow or swag. Examine scraps of lace for usable motifs that can be cut out and added to the card. Of course, embroidery, quilting or other hand stitching is a good way to embellish fabric for a card too. Keep thinking and observing. You will come up with even more ideas, I'm sure.

Stamping & Embossing

"*Nearly all our originality comes from the stamp that time impresses upon our sensibility.*"

—Charles Bauderlaire

Rubber and acrylic stamps allow those of us who cannot draw a straight line the ability to reproduce fine artistic details on our cards. There is a nearly limitless supply of images to be found at craft stores and online. Subject matters range from classical art images to text, from collage arrangements to pets, from flora to insects to … well, you get the idea.

Stamps can be purchased mounted (usually on a wood base) or unmounted. Acrylic blocks allow for easy attachment and removal of unmounted acrylic stamps. The clear blocks and stamps also make it easy to see exactly where the image is being placed on your card.

There are several basic types of inks for use on paper and cardstock. Dye-based ink comes in a variety of rich colors and dries quickly. It is usually not permanent in that moisture can make it run.

Chalk-type ink pads have great colors and can be heat-set to make the print permanent. The finish from a chalk pad has a more opaque look. Pigment ink pads are preferred for embossing. The ink is slow-drying and sticky, allowing it to hold the embossing powder better. There are other specialty inks on the market that are worth investigating as well. Ink pads come in a variety of shapes and sizes.

Embossing powder is actually minute plastic beads that melt when heated. There are heat tools specifically made for embossing. To emboss an image, apply pigment ink to the stamp and press firmly on the desired surface.

The excess can be returned to the embossing powder container. Next, heat the powdered image with an embossing heat tool held above and slightly angled until the powder melts and turns shiny.

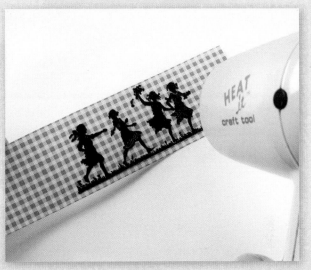

Sprinkle the embossing powder on top of the stamped image; shake off the excess onto a piece of scrap paper.

The heat tool can be moved around as needed to hit all the areas of the image. Take care not to overheat or you may singe the paper. Embossing provides a raised surface to the image, making it easier to add color.

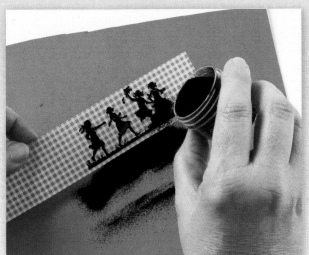

The type of paper or cardstock used to hold a stamped image can affect success. Textured or rough papers make it harder to get a clean, clear image. Smooth papers work much better. Glossy paper or cardstock must be heat-set or embossed for the image to be affixed permanently.

To get a good image, make sure the stamp is inked thoroughly and evenly. The stamp may be pressed into the ink pad or the pad may be pressed onto the stamp. Once the ink is on the stamp, breathe or "huff" on the stamp surface to re-moisten it. Press the stamp firmly onto the paper or cardstock, but do not let it move. It helps to press on a slightly padded surface such as a piece of fun foam that rests on a firm surface. Test on scrap paper first.

Color may be applied to stamped images in several ways. Colored pencils, chalks or pastels applied with foam applicators or cotton swabs, watercolor paints, water-based markers, gel pens, dye-based or alcohol inks applied with a small paintbrush all work very well. Copic® markers are the new coloring agents that are making paper artists swoon. The colors are brilliant and blendable.

Backgrounds for stamping can only be limited by your imagination. The samples shown include cardstock, scrapbooking paper, hand-painted rice paper and torn tissue paper. The autumn leaves were actually stamped onto pages of a magazine, then embossed and cut out. It's also fun to add embellishments to cards with stamped images such as bits of lace or floss, cut-paper motifs or the circles that are left over from a small hole punch. There's even a strip of clipped mesh fabric that, once applied to a circle of fabric, gives the impression of hand stitching.

Stamping Tips

- Store ink pads upside down so the ink will be closer to the top.

- Refurbish embossing pads with a mixture of one part glycerin (found at drugstores) and two parts water.

- Clean stamps using water, baby wipes or stamp cleaner and paper towels.

- Emboss on top of a piece of cardboard covered with aluminum foil to speed up the drying process. The foil reflects the blast of heat back to the cardstock, causing the embossing powder to melt much more quickly.

- Lightly sanding the surface of your new rubber stamps helps them hold the ink better.

One of the most important things to remember about stamping is what your parents used to always tell you: Practice makes perfect!

Pressed Flowers

> *"Talk to me of trillium,*
> *of honeysuckled birds,*
> *or speak of brassy*
> *buttercups. I crave*
> *some April words."*
>
> —Charlotte Corry Partin

The above lines are from the poem *Is April Spoken Here?* by Charlotte Corry Partin. Her book, *Charlotte's Garden*, contains her poetry of the seasons, as well as fantastic pressed-flower art by Kate Chu and May Long.

Pressing flowers to preserve sweet memories of a special occasion has been a centuries-old activity. Pressed leaves and flowers have also served as a way to catalog and identify botanical specimens. Meriwether Lewis and William Clark did just that on their U.S. expedition to find a northwest passage in the early 1800s. There is even a "language of flowers," or floriography, which speaks to the symbolic meanings of individual flowers. For example, red roses symbolize passion, but daisies indicate purity. The language of flowers was popular during Victorian times since one could express sentiments through flowers that would have seemed improper if spoken aloud. For an extensive list of flowers and their meanings, visit www.victorianbazaar.com.

Pressed flowers may also be used in paper arts and card making. Listed here are several easy methods for producing usable botanicals. Remember that blossoms, leaves, grasses, etc. should be picked at their peak of beauty once the dew has evaporated and before the sun causes wilting. If fresh flowers from the garden are not available, a flower shop might be the answer. Usually a florist will allow a viewing of blooms in stock from which individual stems may be purchased. Always obtain permission before picking wildflowers or any other type of botanical on land belonging to someone else.

Pressing Flowers

Using Large Phone Books

Place flowers in between pages and weigh down with heavy books or other weights. A single page can hold several blooms. Make sure the flowers do not touch. Leave about 20 pages or so between each "flower page" to absorb the moisture. Store away from light and moisture. After about two weeks carefully check to see if the botanicals are flat and dry and ready to use. If not, check back on a weekly basis.

Flower Presses

These can be purchased or made. The flowers are pressed between two boards, using cardboard and paper in between. Pressure comes from tightening screws attached to bolts on the boards. Check specimens after one or two weeks.

Microfleur Flower Press

This is a device that uses the microwave oven and is by far the speediest method of pressing flowers. Follow the manufacturer's directions. Most blooms are ready for use the same day. This method also does the best job of preserving color.

Adding Color

Some pressed flowers, such as pansies, keep their colors very well. Other blooms, like impatiens, lose nearly all their pigment. Experimentation is key. Color can sometimes be enhanced by carefully applying pastels (chalks) with a soft brush. Thick flowers, such as roses or marigolds, will press better if the individual petals are separated first from the thick stems.

Using Pressed Flowers in Card Making

Pressed flowers may be grouped together on a card. However, some single blossoms are beautiful enough to stand alone, center stage. Charming "vases" can be made from a scrap of decorative cardstock or piece of tree bark. Painted chipboard frames can set off a lovely portrait of flowers. Handmade paper is also a wonderful complement to the beauty of nature's flora.

It's a good idea to lay out the botanicals on the card to get a pleasing arrangement before attaching them. Adhere flowers to the card or background paper with small dots of white craft glue or use a toothpick or soft paintbrush to apply craft glue.

Needle-nose tweezers are invaluable for moving flowers from the gluing station to their place on the card. Once the flowers are applied, any oozing glue may be gently blotted with a facial tissue.

Tip

For inspiring pressed-flower art check out: www.pressedflowerdesigns.com.

Vintage Images

> "Both actresses and society women find nothing so perfect for hair cleansing as Canthrox Shampoo."
>
> —Pictorial Review, May 1917

"Get your mirror to tell you what your friends will not."

"Noon and Night—float them in bowls of milk—Quaker Puffed Wheat."

"Mellin's Food Method of Milk Modification."

"To keep your hair youthfully dressed, insist on Hump Hair Pins."

These are all advertising slogans from the vintage magazine *Pictorial Review*, May 1917 edition. "Vintage" is an adjective that means "old" or "outmoded" but also is defined as "of recognized and enduring interest, importance or quality. Classic." It is the second part of the definition that applies to the sample cards included here.

There is an endearing quality to antique photos and artwork. Perhaps a memory is stirred of stories our grandparents used to tell us. Perhaps it is imagining a simpler, gentler, more innocent time in human history. Perhaps the cultural style—women used to wear such beautiful hats!—evokes a sense of gentility. Whatever the reason, using vintage images in cards and paper works seems to set them apart as special.

Antique stores and flea markets are great places to find such cultural artifacts. Attics and basements may hold a store of antique photos or magazines. There are online sources containing a treasure trove of images that are copyright free. Two of these websites are www.e-vint.com and www.antiqueclipart.com. Companies such as Artifacts Inc. carry lines of vintage images suitable for use in decoupage. Theirs and similar products can be found at art and craft stores or on the Internet. Periodically public libraries have sales of old books that may be out of copyright too.

Always check the copyright laws to make sure images can be used legally or obtain permission from the copyright holder.

Scraps of lace, torn papers, pressed flowers and vintage pieces of jewelry or small knickknacks can be used to give a card a vintage look.

Self-adhesive gems and pearls can also be added to give a vintage card a more finished, dressed-up look.

It is easy to create cards with vintage imagery. First, select the antique artwork to be featured, and then audition backgrounds and embellishments to complement it. Once the decisions are made, simply glue everything in place with the proper adhesives. Glue sticks work well for lightweight papers while white craft glue or matte medium will secure heavier items in place.

For a dimensional effect, try using foam craft dots.

Text can also be added alongside antique images. Magazines, catalogs, old books or your own handwriting can be sources. There are many computer fonts you can use to generate text as well as rub-on phrases that would coordinate nicely with the classic, vintage look of your card.

Fair warning: Entering the world of vintage imagery may transform you into a treasure hunter, unable to pass an antique store without peeking inside to see what you can find to add to your collection. Enjoy the journey!

Monoprinting

"Creativity is allowing yourself to make mistakes. Art is knowing which one to keep."

—Scott Adams

Snowflakes begin by forming around a speck of dust in the air. After expanding into a tiny hexagonal prism, a snowflake is blown about the sky where wind and temperature make their own contributions to the flake's formation. "No two crystals have the same history, so they don't grow in the same way," states Dr. Kenneth Libbrecht, a physics professor at the California Institute of Technology and author of several books on the art and science of snowflakes. Fabulous images of these wondrous creations can be seen at www.snowcrystals.com.

Monoprints are as unique as snowflakes. They can be similar, as snowflakes can be, but each created pattern gives a singular design that can never be precisely duplicated.

A monoprint is actually a painting that you print yourself. Paint or ink is spread on a nonporous surface such as a plexiglass sheet, metal plate or freezer paper—shiny side up—taped to a work surface. The paint is manipulated to form a design or drawing. A positive print can be taken of the design as is, or a negative image can be printed after removing some of the design via brushes, leaves, string, rubber stamps, etc.

Monoprints can take center stage on a handmade card or make very interesting background papers. Artistic results occur easily and with little effort. Special effects can be achieved by spritzing the painting with water or alcohol before taking the print. The painting can also be "collaged." Different sections can be treated individually—brush strokes in one area, a piece of lace imprinted in another area, text drawn in a third area and so on—before the print is made. "Trace drawings" are made by spreading paint on the nonporous surface, and then laying the paper on top. A finger or other object is used to "draw" on the blank sheet. When the paper is lifted off, the resulting monoprint will likely be a total surprise.

Materials

Glass or plexiglass sheet, metal plate or freezer paper to act as your work surface

Various papers such as watercolor paper, Bristol, drawing paper or rice paper

Hard rubber brayer

Assorted acrylic paints, watercolors and inks

Paintbrushes, combs, toothpicks, bamboo skewers, sponges, leaves and found objects

Spray bottle for water or rubbing alcohol

Drop or spread one or more colors of paint on your work surface. Make a pattern in the paint with paintbrushes or a sponge or swirl in a design with a comb. **Note:** *Other objects such as leaves, toothpicks and bamboo skewers can be used to create unique designs in the paint.*

Try using a texture mat to create a textured pattern in paint.

Place blank sheet of paper on top of painted design. Gently but firmly press with your hands or fingers to make sure pattern is captured onto paper.

A brayer may also be used to help transfer design. **Note:** *A brayer may slightly alter the design depending on thickness of paint—if paint has been thickly applied, the brayer will push the paint around underneath as you roll it across the surface. Nice surprises can happen at this point.*

Carefully remove paper from paint.

You now have produced a monoprint! If there is still enough paint left behind on your work surface, try rolling a brayer over it to create a different pattern that can also be monoprinted. Or spritz with water and lightly move paint with a paintbrush before making another printing. Clean surface as desired between prints so design won't be too muddy.

If the print is not pleasing to the eye, try monoprinting over it again with metallic paint—a bit of gold or silver glitz can really transform a dull print.

Tip

More inspiration and information can be found at www.monoprints.com.

Playing With Pastels

"Some painters transform the sun into a yellow spot; others transform a yellow spot into the sun."

—Pablo Picasso

It has been said that pastels are the most permanent art medium that exists.

Perhaps that is because charcoal is considered a type of pastel, and isn't that what cavemen used for drawing?

Pastels, similar to crafting chalks, can be soft or hard. Soft pastels consist of pure pigment and a binder, usually gum Arabic. Hard pastels are made up of these same ingredients plus kaolin, a type of clay. Soft pastels have more pigment and less binder than the hard variety. The pigments used are the same as those used in all fine art paints. Thus, art that is worked in pastels is called a pastel painting, not a pastel drawing.

Other pastel products include pastel pencils which are the same composition as hard pastels but allow for a finer line. Oil pastels are not chalky at all. They consist of a pigment and wax mix, or non-drying oils in some cases.

Soft and hard pastels are a dry medium, so the colors cannot be premixed as liquid colors can. Instead, they are blended on the canvas or paper often with fingers or a cotton swab. Colors can also be overlaid, one on top of another. The pastels can be fixed in stages or after the painting is finished, though fixatives do darken the colors. Fair warning: Pastels do create a lot of dust; thus they are messy.

It's a good idea to keep damp paper towels or baby wipes close at hand when working with them. Generally pastels are non-toxic, but if respiratory problems are an issue, wearing a mask might be a good idea.

Conventional wisdom says that the choice of paper or other chosen surface is just as important as the pastels themselves in a painting. The paper needs to have enough "tooth," that is texture, to hold the powder to the surface. There are papers made specifically for pastel painting, but others are worth trying. Once the color is laid on the paper, water can be added for a watercolor effect.

Oil pastels can be mixed to a degree before applying them. Baby oil or odorless mineral spirits can be used as a blending agent for the colors either before or after applying.

Creative Ideas to Try With Soft & Hard Pastels

Note: Since soft pastels are easily smudged, it's a good idea to spray all your finished work with a fixative. I use inexpensive hairspray.

Use Pastels With Stencils

Place your stencil as desired and tape down if need be.

Rub the pastel on the tip of your index finger and use it to paint inside the stencil openings. If you want to use multiple colors, you might want to clean your finger with each new color—or not.

Embellish Embossed Images

Stamp and emboss a fairly open image on dark cardstock using a white or light-colored embossing powder. Run a small round paintbrush that has been dipped in water over the top of the pastel, and then paint inside the lines of your stamped image. The colors will lighten as they dry.

Silhouettes

Create a silhouette effect by temporarily adhering a small shape to the center of a piece of light-colored cardstock. Rub a pastel color on your fingertip and place it on the shape. Rub outward from the center of the shape all around it. Remove the shape and

see the silhouette. Larger shapes can be centered and temporarily adhered and then colored in the same manner with a different shade of pastel to create a silhouette within a silhouette.

Backgrounds

Similar to the way silhouettes are created, interesting backgrounds can be created with torn paper and pastels. Start by irregularly tearing a sheet of paper.

Lay torn paper onto background paper and use your fingertip to rub a pastel color along torn edge.

In the same manner, use multiple colors of pastels to create a more colorful background.

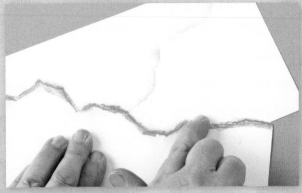

Landscapes

Create an impressionist landscape using pastels and cotton swabs. Have a scene in mind, an image or a painting in front of your workspace for inspiration, and apply color sparingly to a piece of watercolor paper following the scenic guidelines. Pressed flowers or foliage can be added to this to heighten the realism.

Monoprinting

To make a monoprint, make a simple drawing or just apply several colors of pastels to a piece of paper. Spritz with water. Move the colors around, or not, as desired. Lay another blank sheet on top and press with your hands. Lift up the top paper, turn over and reveal your print! Very interesting effects can occur when the pastels are rubbed over an uneven surface such as a piece of textured wallpaper. If there is too much water on the pastel-loaded paper, that's OK—just use an absorbent paper such as watercolor paper for the top sheet and set aside to air dry. The results will likely be even more surprising.

Some Ideas to Try With Oil Pastels

Color Stamped Images

These act a lot like crayons, so use them to color in drawn shapes or open stamped images. Larger images will work best.

Enhance Drawings

Do a drawing with them—such as a flower or piece of fruit—and then add other colors for highlights, smearing them with your fingertip to blend or add a sense of movement. Add other colors to blend in a background.

Sgraffito

Rub the oil pastel heavily over a piece of colored cardstock, and then use a stylus or bamboo skewer to scratch in a design and reveal the color underneath. Alternatively, use metallic markers or several colors of acrylic metallic paint to apply color on a piece of watercolor paper. When dry, rub the oil pastel (black is a good color to use) heavily over the colored area. Scratch in a design to reveal the metallic ink underneath.

Use With Paints

Apply lines of oil pastels to watercolor paper. Then, paint over the lines with watercolor paints or thinned acrylics. The oil pastels will act like a resist.

Experiment and come up with your own techniques!

For further information on using pastels, here are a few websites to check out:

www.how-to-draw-and-paint.com
www.artshow.com
www.ctpastelsociety.com

Eyes
of the
SOUL

Simple Weaving

> *"We sleep, but the loom of life never stops, and the pattern which was weaving when the sun went down is weaving when it comes up in the morning."*
>
> —Henry Ward Beecher

Weaving can be seen many places in nature, from spider webs and caterpillar cocoons to the work of exotic insects and birds. Weaving can even be seen in everyday items, such as textiles, baskets, rag rugs and wire fencing, to name a few. It's easy to see how inspiration for weaving projects can be gained from the world around us.

Weaving is the process of crossing two sets of fibers (or other materials such as metal or paper) over and under each other. The set of fibers that run lengthwise (or vertically) is known as the "warp" fibers. The set of fibers that run crosswise (or horizontally) is known as the "weft" fibers.

Weaving is often done on a loom. A loom is a device which holds the warp threads in place while the weft threads are woven throughout. Some other forms of weaving include tablet weaving, inkle weaving and pin weaving. Then, there is the very simple weaving that is quite easily done and is the subject of this article.

Basic Weaving

Basic, simple weaving can be done with evenly cut strips of paper, fabric, ribbons, yarns, etc. When woven together, a very regular shape of squares will be produced. Alternatively, the paper or fabric strips can be torn unevenly and woven together for a more irregular and artistic effect. Combinations of different materials can be used, such as weaving paper with yarn. Coarse fabric, like burlap, may be used as a base through which to weave narrow ribbons, floss or pearl cotton. Your choice of colors and materials makes all the difference in the look of the finished piece. Experimenting with a wide variety of materials can be quite fun!

Best wishes

Materials

Strips of desired weaving material

Freezer paper (if using paper for weaving)

Fusible interfacing (if using fabric for weaving)

Iron and ironing surface

Scissors or rotary cutter

Ruler

Self-healing cutting mat

Double-sided tape

Masking tape

Basic Weaving Technique

Determine the desired finished size for your woven piece and cut a foundation of freezer paper or fusible interfacing about 1 to 2 inches larger all the way around than the finished measurements.

Place double-sided tape the width of the top edge of the foundation. **Note:** *Freezer paper should be shiny side up when the double-sided tape is applied; the fusible interfacing should be adhesive side up when the double-sided tape is applied.* Attach the warp strips to this, lining them up evenly and butting up against each other with no overlap or gaps.

Begin at the top and weave the weft strips in and out all the way across. On the next row alternate the weave. Continue in this manner down the length of the foundation, making sure that the strips are firmly woven together with no gaps. Place a piece of masking tape across the last woven row to anchor it in place.

Turn the woven piece over on an ironing surface so that the freezer paper or fusible interfacing is on top. With the iron set at medium heat, carefully but firmly iron the foundation to the weaving to set and stabilize it.

Turn the piece right-side up and trim as necessary to fit on the card and adhere.

Lacing Technique

Remember those lace-up or "sewing" cards from elementary school days? Yarn was woven in and out of regularly spaced holes to form a simple shape. That same idea can be applied for use in embellishments for card making. Anything with regularly spaced holes (such as the edges of paper doilies, fabric lace, etc.) can be used to weave ribbon, yarn, etc. for a new or more complex look. Hole punches and some border punches will further allow for lacing holes to be arranged on a multitude of papers and cardstock.

Easy Handmade Paper

"Fill your paper with the breathings of your heart."

—William Wordsworth

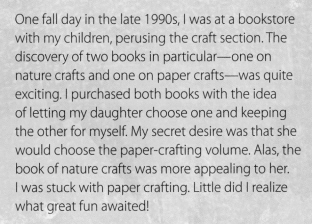

One fall day in the late 1990s, I was at a bookstore with my children, perusing the craft section. The discovery of two books in particular—one on nature crafts and one on paper crafts—was quite exciting. I purchased both books with the idea of letting my daughter choose one and keeping the other for myself. My secret desire was that she would choose the paper-crafting volume. Alas, the book of nature crafts was more appealing to her. I was stuck with paper crafting. Little did I realize what great fun awaited!

In that book, *Papercrafts*, by Gillian Souter, was a chapter on handmade paper, using a blender, scrap paper and a round embroidery hoop with tulle inside for a screen. **Note:** *Make sure that the blender used for paper crafting is not used for food.* It was delightful to find out just how easy it was to turn out beautiful sheets of paper by recycling scraps.

Most any scrap paper can be used to make handmade paper. Blending a variety of scraps will usually produce a pulp in a rather gray shade, but pulp can also be colored (see Coloring Paper Pulp). If a more elegant look is desired (as it was

in making paper for invitations for my son and daughter-in-law's wedding) new, textweight paper can be pulped.

Making Handmade Paper

Materials

Quarter size or shredded pieces of paper	Sponge
Water	100 percent cotton muslin
Blender	Glass baking dish
Large towels	Strainer
Plastic canvas	Bucket or large bowl

Place pieces of paper in a bucket; cover with water and soak for an hour.

Take about a cupful of soaked paper and place in blender. Cover with water 2–3 inches above paper. **Note:** *Do not overwork your blender; add more water when using thicker paper and less water when using lighter paper.* Blend for 15–20 seconds, turning the paper into pulp. Less blending will yield a chunkier paper and more blending will yield a smoother paper. Over blending will result in paper that is too weak.

Cut a piece of plastic canvas and a piece of cotton muslin to desired size. Place plastic canvas into bottom of glass baking dish. Pour paper pulp on top of plastic canvas.

With your fingers, spread the paper pulp evenly over the plastic canvas.

Carefully lift the canvas out of the dish by holding it at diagonal corners and place it on a large folded towel.

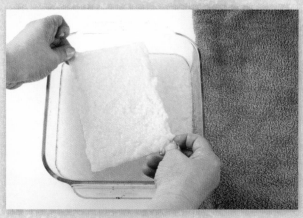

Let the water wick out for a while before placing a piece of muslin on top of another large folded towel. Carefully flip the canvas onto the muslin so that the pulp is sandwiched between the muslin and the plastic canvas.

Using a sponge, carefully brush away all pulp from the edges of the canvas so that it all rests on the muslin. Press the sponge on top of the canvas to remove even more water.

Carefully lift the plastic canvas off of the pulp and lay the pulp-covered piece of muslin aside to dry. Once dry, you have made a piece of paper!

Drain water left in glass baking dish through a strainer to collect leftover paper pulp. This paper pulp can be used to make another sheet of paper, or you can dry or freeze it to use on a future papermaking project.

Warning: *Do not pour paper pulp down a sink drain; it will clog drains. Instead, save pulp for a future project or dry and throw away.*

Tips

- Try using coffee filters, leftover gift wrap, discarded typing sheets or computer paper, card inserts from magazines, leftover, fast-food napkins and tea bag papers to make handmade papers.

- Do not use newspaper, full-color magazines, vellum and other plastic product or foil wrappers to make handmade papers.

- Speed-dry paper sheets by placing another piece of muslin on top of wet paper sheet and iron it dry using a hot iron.

Coloring Paper Pulp

To color paper pulp, add colored construction paper, colored bond paper, brightly colored party napkins or highly pigmented flower petals (such as pansies or geraniums) to the blender at the same time as the paper pieces. Bond and construction paper should be soaked a little first, but the others can be added with no soaking.

Adding Texture to Paper Pulp

Add flower petals, dried flowers and leaves, leftover tea bags (remove staples), herbs or corn silk to blender at the same time as paper pieces. It is even possible to add wildflower seeds to the paper pulp. Later, the seeded paper can be planted. Seeded paper makes an interesting addition to a handmade card given to a friend.

Nature Prints

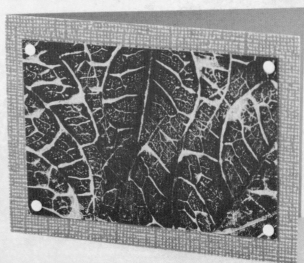

> *"What a nature printer needs most is a combination of curiosity and patience."*
>
> —Robert W. Little, author, *Nature Printing*

Nature offers myriad works of art without the fear of breaking copyright laws. We may freely partake of this proffered beauty by employing the technique of nature printing. Precise reproductions are achievable. You only need some botanical specimens plus a few supplies.

Small single leaves or blooms can lead the viewer of your finished piece of art to take a closer, more appreciative look at a plant that might not be considered beautiful in its own right—such as a weed. Or, several elements can be arranged to suit your individual taste. Printing with several leaves can produce elegant backgrounds for small cards.

If you don't have a garden or yard of your own from which to glean, try the produce aisle at the local grocery store. Parsley, cilantro, celery leaves, spinach or baby lettuce are a few of the choices available there. Additional places to look are local flower shops, greenhouses and home improvement stores that sell plants and flowers.

Tips Before Beginning

- Make sure the botanical is fresh and dry, but not wilted.

- If sturdy enough, several printings can be obtained from one leaf, petal or blossom.

- Sometimes the leaf can be rehydrated by placing it in a bowl of water for a minute to make it last longer.

- Spring is the very best time for leaves to have prominent veining on their undersides, which makes for excellent printing. Other seasons will work, too, with a different effect.

- Single petals from very full flowers might be easier to print than the entire flower. To still give the effect of a full flower, print with a single petal multiple times, drying between each print.

Materials

Fresh leaves or flowers
Acrylic paints
2 foam trays
Small flat paintbrush or
    soft rubber brayer
Newspaper or towel

Absorbent papers such
    as watercolor paper,
    rice paper or printing
    paper
Waxed paper
Needle-nose tweezers

Note: *Watercolors, watercolor pencils or colored pencils can be used in place of the acrylic paints.*

Nature Printing Technique

Protect work surface with newspaper or similar material. Lay paper to be printed onto the protected work surface.

Make a small puddle of acrylic paint on the foam tray. Using a dry paintbrush, apply a thin layer of paint onto side of leaf with most prominent texture.

Gently place the painted side of the leaf on top of your paper. Cover leaf with waxed paper. Using fingers, gently but firmly press all areas of the leaf.

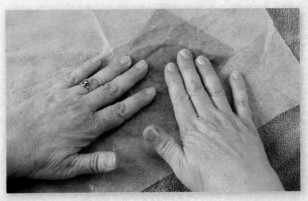

Carefully remove waxed paper. Using tweezers, remove leaf from paper and admire your print!

Optional: *Once print is thoroughly dry, it may be enhanced with color by painting or using colored pencils or pastels.*

Flower Pounding

Another method of printing with nature is flower pounding. By using a hammer or hard rubber mallet, the natural pigment is extracted from the botanical and transferred to desired absorbent paper. In other words, the plant "paints" a picture of itself with your help.

Working on a hard, protected surface, place your flower or leaf on desired absorbent paper and cover with waxed paper. With hammer or hard rubber mallet, firmly pound the botanical.

Remove the waxed paper and remains of the botanical to see the print you have made.

This technique requires a fair amount of experimentation to see which botanicals will transfer the best. There are many variables that will affect success, such as how much pigment the plant contains, how dry or moist it is, and how old the specimen was when picked, to name a few.

In my experience, geraniums and peonies have too much pigment and make a splattered mess when pounded. Impatiens and camellias have almost no pigment and barely show up as beige marks on the paper. Some that produce great results are pansies, verbena, Japanese maple, periwinkle and some ferns. Again, experimentation is the order of the day.

There are several excellent books on nature printing as well as flower pounding. Check with your local library or bookstore. There are also some tutorials for flower pounding on YouTube.

For inspiration for nature printing, check out www.natureprintingsociety.info for a much wider range of nature printing.

Dogwood

Embroidery & Hand-Stitching

> *"I cannot count my day complete, 'Til needle, thread and fabric meet."*
>
> —Author Unknown

"A man at work, making something which he feels will exist because he is working at it and wills it, is exercising the energies of his mind and soul as well as of his body. Memory and imagination help him as he works. Not only his own thoughts, but the thoughts of the men of past ages guide his hands; and, as part of the human race, he creates. If we work thus, we shall be men, and our days will be happy and eventful."
—*William Morris (1834-1896)*

Hand embroidery can be creative work. Such was mentioned in the quote from William Morris, a British artist, writer and printer best known for his beautifully designed textiles. Embroidery is a happy pastime. The multitude of colors to be found in floss is a joy. Line and texture are stimulating. The stitching itself is calming and relaxing. The designs for embroidery can be simple or sophisticated.

Pattern inspiration is everywhere—nature, architecture, tile floors, jewelry designs, anything with a decorative element, as well as in numerous books and online resources. Even your own doodles can provide a design for stitching. Embroidery need not be time-consuming. Modest motifs might require only a few minutes. Complex work can take many hours. The choice is yours.

The embroidery on the sample cards is quite casual, using simple stitches that are worked in a freehand style. Because the scraps of fabric are quite small, no hoops were used. If your comfort level demands a hoop, the scrap can be basted to a larger piece of fabric and then worked in a hoop or frame. Patterns can be drawn on, traced or designed spontaneously.

Designs printed on cloth can also be embroidered, as shown in three of the samples. In all of these cases, the printed fabric was stabilized with iron-on interfacing before the embroidery was worked. Beads add interesting touches, as do pieces of vintage lace. Even the tiniest scraps can be randomly placed and ironed onto freezer paper or other iron-on stabilizers, covered with tulle, and stitched with metallic thread in a simple line design.

Backgrounds for embroidery provide another opportunity for an artistic touch. While plain muslin, cottons and linens are sufficient, hand-dyed fabrics such as batiks—or a leftover scrap of home decor fabric—might be much more interesting, if the embroidery design allows. Scrapbook papers are fun to use too, with an embroidered piece of fabric glued on top.

Included here are some hand-stitching diagrams.

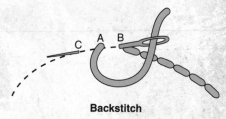

Backstitch

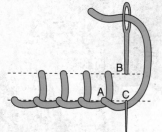

Buttonhole Stitch

Chain Stitch

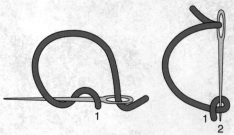

French Knot

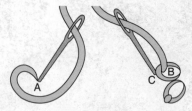

Lazy-Daisy Stitch

Satin Stitch